DISCOVERY IN EGYPT

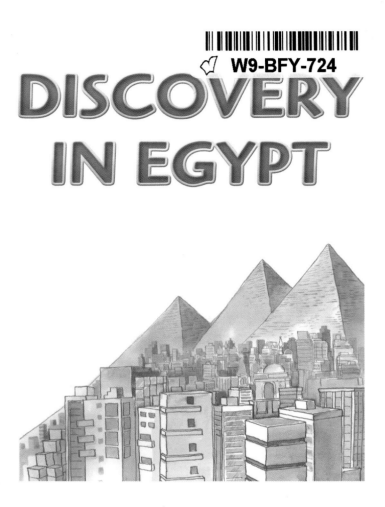

Jonny Zucker
Illustrated by Ronald Lipking

Rigby
A Harcourt Achieve Imprint

www.Rigby.com
1-800-531-5015

Literacy by Design Leveled Readers: *Discovery in Egypt*

ISBN-13: 978-1-4189-3915-1
ISBN-10:   1-4189-3915-3

Printed in China
4 5 6 7 8 0940 14 13 12 11 10 09

CONTENTS

Chapter 1

THE CITY OF CAIRO

Tyrone and Serena Turner were going on an adventure. The eleven-year-old twins and their mom were on a plane headed to Cairo, Egypt. Their mother, Angela Turner, was an archaeologist. She studied ancient Egypt.

After years of begging, Tyrone and Serena were joining her on her latest journey to Egypt. Whenever they had asked before, their parents said, "We'll just have to see." That almost always meant *no*.

This year, however, the twins' dad, Bradley Turner, was touring the United States, giving lectures about Egypt. So the twins got to leave Boston, Massachusetts, for the wonder of Cairo, Egypt.

"It's not going to be nonstop fun," Mom had warned the twins. "I'll be working most of the time."

"That's OK!" said Tyrone. "We'll help you solve all sorts of mysteries!"

Once the plane landed, the family got a taxi. Mom told the driver to drop them off at their hotel.

"Stop laying on me!" Serena said, pushing Tyrone's head off her shoulder.

"I'm tired!" Tyrone complained. "The plane ride was fifteen hours long!"

When they reached the hotel, they had just enough energy to take their luggage up to their room before falling asleep.

"What would you two like to see first?" Mom asked the next morning. "We don't have to leave for the camp yet, so we have time to explore."

"I want to see the pyramids in Giza," Tyrone said.

"And the Sphinx," Serena added.

"All right," said Mom. "We'll go there after breakfast."

Before they'd even left the city of Cairo, they could see three pyramids towering against the clear blue sky. The closer they got to the town of Giza, the more magnificent the pyramids looked.

"There's so much going on!" said Serena when they reached the town. The three of them made their way slowly through the mass of people around them. People were selling all sorts of things—cloth dyed beautiful colors, strange-looking fruit, and all kinds of pottery. The scent of food and perfume filled the air.

The Turners bought some sweet pastries and snacked on them as they walked closer to the pyramids.

"The largest pyramid is the Great Pyramid," Mom said, pointing to the closest one. "It was built around 2580 B.C."

"It's almost five thousand years old. That's amazing!" said Tyrone. They were standing at the base of the Great Pyramid now, and it seemed to stretch above them endlessly.

"Now let's go see the Sphinx," Serena said excitedly. They headed toward the imposing statue, which had the body of a lion and the head of a human. The head was missing its nose.

"It looks like it's protecting something," said Tyrone.

Suddenly he noticed an old woman staring at them intently. "Look," Tyrone whispered to Serena. "That woman is staring at us."

"Just ignore her," Serena answered, so he did. They both forgot about her for the rest of the day.

The next day they went to the Egyptian Museum. The twins were overwhelmed by how much the museum held. "I love this museum," Mom said. "Each time there's more to discover. I have old favorites I like to revisit, too, like this statue." She paused in front of a statue with the body of a lion and the head of a human.

"It looks like the Sphinx," Serena said.

"Yes," Mom said, "This one has the face of Hatshepsut, a female pharaoh."

"But the face has a beard!" Tyrone said.

"Hatshepsut wore male clothing and a false beard," Mom continued. "The beard was a symbol reminding people of Osiris, the ancient Egyptians' most important god."

The Turners gradually made their way to the display on Tutankhamen, a pharaoh of ancient Egypt. Despite the lateness of the day, there was a huge crowd.

"Tutankhamen was very young when he became the pharaoh of Egypt," said Mom. "In fact, he was younger than you: just nine years old. His tomb was discovered by Howard Carter. It had sat almost untouched for three thousand years."

"What do you mean, 'almost'?" asked Tyrone, confused.

"Many of the tombs were found by robbers," Mom said. "They would sell whatever they could. For some reason, the robbers didn't take much from Tutankhamen's tomb. So when Howard Carter discovered it in 1922, everything inside was almost as it had been when Tutankhamen was buried."

"It must have been amazing to discover an unknown tomb!" Serena said as she looked at everything discovered in the tomb, jewelry and sculptures and furniture. Just then she thought she saw a familiar figure. "Tyrone," she whispered, "isn't that the woman who was staring at us yesterday?"

"I think you're right," he whispered back. "Do you think she's following us?"

"There's only one way to find out," Serena answered. She walked over to the old woman. "Excuse me," she said, "can we help you?"

The old woman smiled at her. "No," she said, "but I can help you." She handed Serena a package wrapped in brown cloth. When Serena looked up from the package, the old woman had disappeared.

"Who was that?" Mom asked, coming up behind Serena and Tyrone.

"I don't know, but she gave us this," Serena said, handing the small package to her mother.

"How strange," Mom said as she gently unwrapped it. "This is a very rare and unusual amulet!"

"What's an amulet?" asked Tyrone.

"It's a charm that ancient Egyptians wore around their necks," explained Serena. "They thought it brought them luck."

The amulet was a round disc that looked like a beetle, with a colored stone for its body. "I would love to ask her where she got this," Mom said. The three of them searched the museum, but the old woman had vanished.

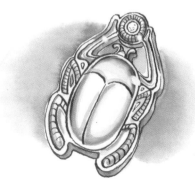

"It's our first mystery!" said Serena.

They continued to walk around, stopping in front of a display of an ancient Egyptian mummy. "This reminds me of Dad," said Serena.

The twins both loved listening to their father explain how the ancient Egyptians created mummies. They had heard his lecture so many times that they could repeat it easily.

"First, the body was washed," Tyrone began, mocking his father's serious voice.

Serena grinned at him and continued, "Then the internal organs, such as the lungs and stomach, were removed. The ancient Egyptians thought that intelligence was kept inside the heart, so it was left in the body."

"The other organs were washed and packed in jars, which were kept in the tomb with the mummy." This was Tyrone's favorite part.

"Next the body was covered with salt to dry it out. After forty days, the body was washed again and covered in oil," Serena cleared her throat at this point, something their father always did.

Not to be outdone, Tyrone pushed pretend glasses up his nose. "Next the body was wrapped in cloth. Each layer of wrapping was covered with resin, a thick fluid made by certain plants. The resin was very sticky so that the wrappings would stay in place."

"The entire process took about seventy days," the twins finished together.

Their mother laughed. "You two are just too much."

After the museum, the family stopped at a restaurant to eat. While they were enjoying their meal of spiced meat, bread, and dipping sauces, they talked about what they'd seen at the museum, wondering about the strange old woman who'd given them the amulet.

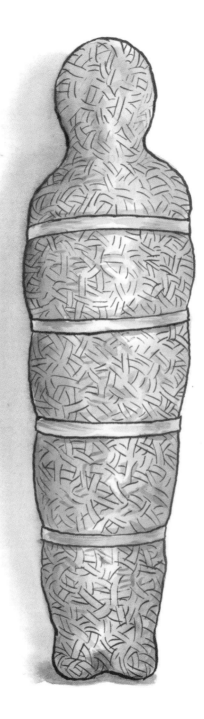

After they finished their meal, the family headed back to the hotel. They had to get up early the next morning to get ready to head to the camp, so everyone wanted to get plenty of sleep.

Chapter 2

GOING TO CAMP

The next afternoon, the Turners left their hotel and headed for the bus stop. They passed people selling sweet-smelling pastries and beautiful jewelry and a group of children playing soccer with an old leather ball before they finally reached the bus stop.

Ten minutes later, an old bus rattled round the corner and came to a sputtering stop. The driver was a bearded man with a huge grin. He led the three waiting passengers on board and pointed to the back where the only empty seats were. Then they were off to the camp.

Their driver swerved and skidded skillfully, beeping his horn and chewing sunflower seeds. After about an hour, the bus left the buildings and streets of the city and headed out onto the dusty plain.

By the time the Turners arrived at the camp, it was dark outside. They were surprised to find that they were the only passengers left on the bus. They climbed off sleepily, and the warm night air hit them like a heavy blanket. The driver dragged their bags out of the cargo hold, waved goodbye, and then rumbled off into the night.

The Turners found themselves standing at the entrance to a large, circular village of tents surrounded by huge trees. "Some of the larger tents are for research and working on what we've found out at the archaeological site. Others are for storage, cooking, and dining. The smaller tents are for people to sleep in," Mom explained as she led the twins around the camp.

She stopped outside a large tent. The lights shining inside outlined two figures against the canvas of the tent. "Here we are," said Mom as she opened the tent flap and led Serena and Tyrone inside. "I want you to meet some people I work with."

Facing them were two men, one tall and thin, with a black moustache and beard and kind eyes, and the other short and squat, with a heavily wrinkled forehead and an intense look in his eyes.

The men were holding a small piece of stone up to the light of an oil lamp. It was a large tile decorated with green ovals and blue and red semi-circles.

As soon as the Turners entered the tent, the men turned to greet them.

"Welcome, Angela! We've missed you," said the taller man. "And you two must be Serena and Tyrone."

"Hello, Henry," said Mom. She turned to Serena and Tyrone. "This is Dr. Henry Singh, an archaeologist from England. We've been working together for years."

"I'm Dr. Sharp," the smaller man said, "and I'm in charge of this dig. We've never had children on site before, but Dr. Turner has assured me that you two are extremely well behaved. So I'm sure we won't have any problems from you."

"Oh, don't be such a grump, George," Dr. Singh looked at Dr. Sharp fondly. "They're Angela and Bradley's children. They'll be perfect."

Dr. Sharp frowned and carried the tile across the tent to a low table covered in magnifying glasses and microscopes.

"Don't worry about him," grinned Dr. Singh. "He's completely wrapped up in his work."

Mom smiled back at Dr. Singh. "It's good to see you two again," she said, "but I think the three of us are going to bed now. We'll see you in the morning."

"Goodnight, Dr. Singh. Goodnight, Dr. Sharp," the twins said as their mother led them out of the tent.

The Turners' tent was just tall enough for them to stand without their heads touching the ceiling. There were three mattresses, each one with a mosquito net over it. An oil lamp hung from the central tent pole. A few tables were next to the mattresses.

"Well," said Mom, "this seems pretty comfortable. It's going to be home for the next week, so let's try to keep it neat."

Serena and Tyrone shot glances at each other that said the tent wasn't exactly what they'd call *comfortable*.

They placed their suitcases in one corner of the tent and their backpacks on the bedside tables. Then they followed Mom to a tent where they could brush their teeth and get ready for bed.

"Breakfast time," Mom said, waking the twins the next morning. Serena and Tyrone were sure they had closed their eyes only minutes before.

Serena checked her watch and protested sleepily, "But it's only 5 a.m." Tyrone could only grumble in agreement.

"Of course it is! That's the whole point," Mom laughed. "We work at the site early in the morning before the day gets too hot, then we have lunch and maybe a nap, and when it cools down later, we go back to do more work."

Still half asleep, the twins grumpily got dressed. Ten minutes later, they found themselves in the dining tent, where all the meals were served.

Dr. Singh waved the Turners over to his table. "Grab some food and come and sit with me."

When they'd finished eating their breakfast, they all piled into a jeep. Dr. Singh drove them to the archaeological site, which was two miles from the camp.

Even though it was early, the site was already buzzing with activity. A group of young people (college students volunteering during their vacation, Mom said) was digging in a wide hole, and a photographer was leaning over a small wooden table, taking pictures of a large rounded stone.

The site was just a large rectangle stretching out across the desert. It was surrounded by ropes and had different-sized holes dug in it.

The site stood about four hundred feet away from a mountain range. There was no shade, so it was very hot.

After only a few minutes of walking around in the heat, Tyrone and Serena missed all of the trees at the camp. Although the heat was unpleasant, none of the archaeologists seemed to mind too much. Serena and Tyrone stood in awe, watching all the archaeologists at work.

Chapter 3

HELPING HANDS

The Turners toured the site until Mom spotted Dr. Sharp studying a large map. He nodded to Mom but barely noticed the twins, too focused on his work to see them standing next to her.

"OK, I'm going to be working now," said Mom. "You two play with the books, games, and puzzles in your backpacks.

"Go and make yourselves at home in the first aid tent," she directed, pointing to a large white tent with a red cross on its door. "Try to stay cool, and remember to drink plenty of water. If you need me, just come out and find me or ask someone to get me."

The first aid tent contained a bed, a large collection of bottled water, medical equipment, and two green hard plastic chairs, which Serena and Tyrone immediately claimed.

It was still early, but it was already uncomfortably hot inside the tent. Serena opened her backpack and took out a book of crossword puzzles.

"This is not what I imagined when I thought of helping Mom on her dig," Serena said, frowning.

"No kidding," agreed Tyrone as he began working on a crossword puzzle.

Time passed very slowly. By 10:30 a.m., they were getting a bit restless and were relieved when Mom came in to take them to camp for lunch.

In the dining tent, they ate a light lunch of peanut butter sandwiches and dried fruit. Tyrone and Serena hadn't expected to feel so drowsy after eating, but shortly after they went back to their tent, they were both fast asleep.

After a long nap, the twins woke up feeling refreshed, and by 4:00 p.m. they were back at the site. Thankfully, the first aid tent was far cooler in the afternoon than in the morning.

"I can't do any more crossword puzzles," Tyrone groaned.

"Here," said Serena. "Let's draw." She fished around in her backpack and pulled out a couple of pads and some art pens. She and Tyrone spent the afternoon drawing and reading. They were keeping out of the way as they had been told, but they felt increasingly useless and bored for the rest of the day.

The next morning it was the same. Serena and Tyrone found themselves back in the first aid tent searching through their backpacks for something fun to do.

They were in the middle of complaining to each other again when Mom appeared. "You've been so good in here," she said, "and I know you must be very bored. I was wondering if you'd like to come and help me out a little. I think I've finally convinced Dr. Sharp that you won't break anything."

"Definitely!" Tyrone said.

Mom led them to a long wooden table, which held many fragments that had been dug up but were not yet identified.

"OK," Mom instructed, "here's a brush for each of you. These fragments need to be carefully dusted. Hopefully, you'll be able to see if these fragments are pieces of pottery or of tiles. Put them into one of two piles, pottery or tile. If you're not sure if something is pottery or tile, just set it off to the side and ask me about it later."

"This is pretty cool," Serena said, happy about their task. "Just think–these pieces were touched by ancient Egyptians!"

"Yeah," Tyrone said. "That's pretty cool. But more importantly, this is about a million times better than sitting in the first aid tent." They both laughed.

As the twins continued working, the fierce sun beat down onto them. The air of the desert was so hot, they were glad they had hats and plenty of water to drink.

"Hello, you two," said a friendly voice.

"Hi, Dr. Singh," said Tyrone and Serena, happy to see a friendly face.

"I was wondering whether you two would like to take a break," Dr. Singh said. "You've been doing a good job dusting these. It's because of work like this that we understand so much about ancient Egypt."

Dr. Singh carefully picked up a fragment. "It's important that we look at everything we find at a site. That way we have a more complete picture of what life was like for people who lived in ancient Egypt."

Just then, Mom showed up. "Hello, Dr. Singh," she said, "I was just coming to check on the twins. How are you doing?" she asked Tyrone and Serena.

"We're doing OK," Serena said.
"Dr. Singh was just telling us how important
our work is."

"I was going to see if you wanted to bring
them with us tomorrow when we explore the
mountain," Dr. Singh said to Mom.

Tyrone and Serena looked at each other
in excitement. "What's at the mountain?"
asked Tyrone.

"We have another site out there," Mom answered.

"Please, can we go?" asked Serena.

"I don't know, Serena. I'll have to talk to Dr. Sharp," Mom said. "But if he says it's OK with him, I would love for you to join us."

Chapter 4
AN AMAZING SITE

The next morning Serena and Tyrone could barely contain their excitement. Dr. Sharp had agreed to let them go to the second site that day. They all piled into a jeep, and Dr. Singh drove them to the second site, with another jeep of archaeologists following them.

The second site stretched to the base of one of the mountains. Mom stopped at one of the roped-off holes. "We'll be right here. You two can hang around and watch us, or you can go exploring on your own. But don't go into any caves, and always keep us in sight. Do you have your bottled water?"

"Yes, Mom," Serena said.

"Don't worry," said Tyrone. "We'll be fine."

The twins spent the morning wandering around the site. After a few hours, everyone started to get ready to go back to the camp for lunch. "Come on," Mom called. "Time for us to go."

"I'll race you to the jeep," Tyrone said.

"You're on!" Serena replied, jumping up and racing off toward the jeep. She hadn't gone very far before her foot hit something, sending her tumbling.

"Ouch!" said Serena as she hit the ground with a thud. Tyrone immediately ran back to her.

"Are you OK?" he asked.

"Yeah, I'm fine," Serena said, starting to get up. Something unusual about the dirt by her knee caught her eye, though. Carefully she brushed away the dirt to reveal a dirty, ancient-looking disc. She and Tyrone stared at it.

The disc looked like a beetle with a colored stone for its body. "Tyrone, it's like that amulet the old woman gave us!" Serena said. "We should show this to Mom."

"Mom, we found something!" Tyrone yelled in excitement.

Mom quickly walked over to them. Her eyes grew wide in amazement. "That looks important," she said. "Dr. Singh, come here and see what Tyrone and Serena found!"

37

"How remarkable!" said Dr. Singh. "This is a rare amulet. It's in the shape of a scarab beetle, which was important to the ancient Egyptians."

"Mom, doesn't this look like the amulet that woman gave us?" Tyrone asked.

"You're right!" Mom exclaimed. "I can't believe I'd forgotten about that!" She reached into her backpack and pulled out the amulet. She compared it to the amulet Serena was holding. They looked alike.

"Very strange!" Dr. Singh said after the Turners told him the story of the amulet. "These amulets are particularly interesting because they don't fit in with the rest of the pieces that we've found."

"So you think both amulets came from the same site?" Serena asked.

"It certainly looks like it," Dr. Singh said. "I'll take these amulets back to have a closer look at them. I'm sure Dr. Sharp will be excited about this as well."

Dr. Singh was right–Dr. Sharp was nearly speechless when he saw the amulets. After the twins told the story of the old woman again, he asked them where exactly they'd found the second amulet.

Dr. Sharp said, "You were very lucky to discover this." He suddenly grinned at the twins. It was the first time they had seen him smile. "Maybe having you two here wasn't such a bad idea."

Back in their tent that night, the twins tried to convince their mom to let them do more exploring.

"We found that amulet," said Tyrone. "Who knows what else is out there waiting for us? Please, Mom!"

"You did really well today," Mom said. "And you both are very observant. I'm especially proud of you for remembering about that amulet you were given. You might be able to help some more."

"But what about exploring?" asked Serena.

Mom replied with the phrase that the twins hated. "We'll just have to see."

The next day at breakfast, Serena and Tyrone waited impatiently to hear whether they could go back to the mountains.

"I have good news for you," Dr. Singh said. "Your mother and I talked with Dr. Sharp, and he has no problems with the two of you coming out to the mountains again. He seems to think that you're good luck."

Serena and Tyrone were overjoyed to head out toward the mountain site again with the other archaeologists. Visions of amazing discoveries danced through their minds.

When they finally arrived, Mom pointed to the mountain range. "Because of where you found the amulet, we're going to examine those caves," she said, "so our adventure will begin over there."

"Excellent!" grinned Tyrone, more than ready to begin exploring.

Everyone walked toward the mountains, a cool morning breeze gently blowing in their faces. As the twins neared the range, they saw the caves at its base.

Late that afternoon, after the twins had given up hope of finding anything exciting, Mom let out a happy cry. "Come look at this, you two," she said. Tyrone and Serena ran over, along with several archaeologists.

Mom pointed at the stone wall of a cave. "Do you see that?" she asked.

As Tyrone looked closely at the stone, he noticed something unusual. "Hey, Serena, what are all these weird squiggly marks?" Tyrone asked.

"They're hieroglyphs, or symbols," said Serena, "ancient Egyptian writing. Each picture means something different."

"And if I'm reading these hieroglyphs correctly," Mom said, "then this is the entrance to a pharaoh's tomb."

"No way!" said Tyrone.

"I think we may have discovered something amazing," Mom said with a huge smile.

"What are we going to do now?" asked Serena. The other archaeologists were talking excitedly to each other.

"It's going to be dark soon and we have to get back," Mom replied. "We must continue this adventure tomorrow."

The twins groaned in disappointment, but they didn't argue. The other archaeologists seemed disappointed, too. Even Mom looked like she didn't want to leave the cave.

The Turners drove back to camp with Dr. Singh, talking nonstop about the amazing discovery. Once they arrived at camp, news of their discovery traveled quickly.

Dr. Singh smiled at the twins. "Everyone is talking about the tomb, but I think the best find has been you two!" he said. "One day you'll make brilliant archaeologists, just like your mother!"

During their dinner in the dining tent, Dr. Sharp walked over to them and sat down. "This might be the best find since Howard Carter discovered the tomb of Tutankhamen," he said in awe.

"This is where those amulets must have come from," added Dr. Singh. "They must have belonged to the pharaoh buried here. I wonder how that woman you met ended up with that amulet."

"Yeah," Tyrone said, "and why did she give it to us? Did she know it could help us discover the tomb?"

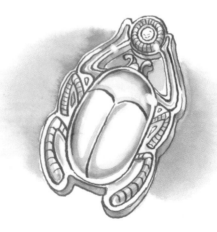

"I suppose we'll never know," Dr. Singh said. "The more you participate in these digs, the more you realize that some mysteries will probably never be solved."

Chapter 5

BACK TO BOSTON

When summer was over, the twins and their mother flew back to Boston. They told their father every detail of their amazing trip. He was as proud of them as their mother was. "I think you've discovered your destiny," he said. "Obviously the two of you are meant to be archaeologists!"

As time passed, it seemed like their time in Egypt had been a dream. But Serena and Tyrone didn't forget how it had felt to discover something amazing.

One night Mom gathered the whole family in front of the television. "I have something very exciting to show you," she said, turning on the international news. In a few moments, they saw a familiar face.

Dr. Singh was addressing a huge audience in Cairo. "Earlier this year, an amazing discovery was made. In a cave within some mountains outside of Cairo, the tomb of a lost pharaoh was discovered."

Camera flashes went off and questions were shouted.

Dr. Sharp, who was sitting beside Dr. Singh, continued. "While we are both very experienced archaeologists, we cannot take the credit for this remarkable find ourselves.

"At first I was against having children on site for this dig," explained Dr. Sharp, "but now I'm delighted they came. You see," he went on, "this discovery must actually be credited to our coworker, Dr. Angela Turner, and her children, Serena and Tyrone."

The Turner family cheered. Serena and Tyrone jumped up and down. The entire family was laughing and hugging. "Wow!" said Serena. "I guess Dr. Sharp liked us after all!"

Mom laughed. "Yes, you certainly won him over. This is a huge discovery!"

"Does that mean we'll be helping you from now on?" asked Serena.

"After all," said Tyrone, "we are your good-luck charms."

Mom and Dad said those familiar words the twins hated to hear. "We'll just have to see."

This time, however, the twins didn't mind. They knew it was just a matter of time before they would be back in Egypt, uncovering more mysteries.